slum dogs of india

Eloise Leyden

slum dogs of india

MERRELL
LONDON · NEW YORK

Contents

slum dogs of india

Introduction

I planned my trip to India after graduating with a degree in photography from the University of Plymouth in southern England. Dogs have long been a passion in my life, so the prospect of exploring this wonderful country through the eyes of its canine population seemed like not only a logical idea but also a positively beguiling one. I set off with my boyfriend (or unpaid assistant) and my trusty camera (a 1970s Pentax) in August 2007.

All life takes place on the streets of India. People work, eat, sleep, wash and socialize there. Alongside the people are the animals: dogs and cows predominantly, but also cats, monkeys, goats, pigs, donkeys and chickens; all form part of the rich fabric of Indian street life. I've always felt that it's good for the soul to be surrounded by animals; it reminds us that humans are just one of many species making their way in the world. Well, if animals are good for the soul, then India is good for the soul.

India is a land where outstanding natural beauty coexists with naked human misery, where rich meets poor, and life-affirming compassion meets maddening indifference. It is a country steeped in tradition, culture and religion, falling over itself to embrace the modern and the new. It is a place of ancient gods and iPods. It is the Third World in conflict with the First. This series of photographs was my attempt to explore India and especially to represent the dogs living on every street corner. The images in this book are the product of a long-standing fascination with and admiration for dogs, my celebration of the unique beauty, spirit and colour that they bring to the world.

Most free-roaming dogs in India belong to an ancient breed known as the Pariah dog. The breed has thrived for around 14,000 years, and the diversity that exists today is the result of Pariahs breeding with pedigree and cross-breed dogs that have been introduced as pets. Pariahs have always been scavengers, living on the detritus created by human beings.

Planning my trip, I was apprehensive about the state in which I would find these stray dogs. The answer, I soon

Opposite: Serena treats the permanent residents at TOLFA in Pushkar, Rajasthan. Dogs that for a variety of reasons cannot be returned to the street stay at the shelter to live out their days.

Above: Sharda prepares the daily food for the dogs, ably assisted by permanent resident Squirrel.

discovered, was completely varied. Some dogs were brimming with health; others were seriously ill. Their temperaments also covered the whole spectrum, from ultra-friendly to downright vicious.

I found that the Indian people's treatment of dogs generally fell into one of three categories: there are the compassionate ones, who love and care for their animals, providing shelter and food. Then there are those who treat the strays as vermin to be chased away, beaten or exterminated. The vast majority, however, occupy an apathetic middle ground. They accept the presence of the dogs as a reality of life and, while never condescending to touch or pet one, might toss it the occasional scrap of food or allow it to sleep unchallenged on their doorstep. It generally follows that dogs that are used to positive, loving contact from humans are friendly, while those that are beaten, shunned or mistreated turn out to be extremely fearful or, if provoked, vicious.

Although in many cases stray dogs – when left to their own devices – do in fact thrive, benefiting from the freedom that a life on the streets allows, the problems associated with strays are numerous. Rabies remains a major threat to public health across the subcontinent and may explain much of the animosity directed towards the dogs by humans. Added to this are the logistical and philosophical dilemmas of providing consistent animal welfare across a country as large and ultimately as poor as India.

Below: Blind dog David, who cannot be returned to the street, finds a bed all of his own in a corner of the shelter.

Opposite, top: Rachel, TOLFA's founder, works on the streets of Pushkar with Annu and Manoj, in a regular mobile clinic treating dogs for mange and tick infestation.

Opposite, bottom: This young resident came to the shelter with paralysed back legs. His condition slowly improved until he was fully mobile on all four legs.

Two very different methods of dealing with these issues have emerged. In certain states – notably Kerala, and Jammu and Kashmir – authorities sweep through, either poisoning or barbarically rounding up strays. Unfortunately, death by lethal injection is considered too expensive, and the variety of ways in which the dogs are destroyed ranges from the cruel to the horrific. There are numerous reasons, other than the obvious ethical ones, to suggest this approach is ineffective.

The cities of Jaipur and Mumbai, among others, adopt a different approach. There, a highly progressive and successful scheme of sterilization and inoculation controls the stray population in a humane way. Both male and female dogs are neutered and a rabies jab is administered at the same time. A nick in the ear or a brand on the leg prevents any dog from being captured twice. In this way, the number of strays is kept in check, very sick animals are put to sleep humanely and the spread of rabies is contained.

With sterilization, the stray population becomes stable and decreases over time. It also becomes largely non-aggressive. On the other hand, when strays are killed or forcibly removed from an area, new dogs keep arriving; the population continuously multiplies and changes, and thus becomes unstable and aggressive. Fighting among the dogs exacerbates the spread of rabies, not just within the stray population, but also possibly among humans too. Although

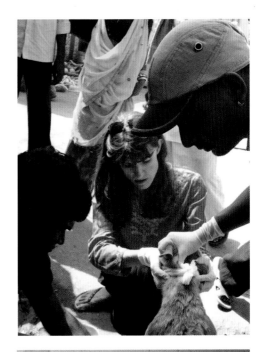

Siteram bonds with one of the charges housed in a block for abandoned and orphaned puppies.

it is illegal to kill a stray animal in India, bribery and legal loopholes have allowed the activity to remain commonplace.

Pushkar and Ajmer, in the state of Rajasthan, are other cities that control the dog population through sterilization or Animal Birth Control (ABC). In Pushkar, as in several other locations across the country, a foreigner who witnessed the plight of stray animals has set up an animal hospital and shelter. The Tree of Life for Animals (TOLFA) was established by an English woman called Rachel Wright. TOLFA's goal is to control the dog population humanely by the ABC method, as well as to provide veterinary care for any animal that needs it, but particularly homeless animals. In addition, it aims to educate and foster compassion in local people about animal welfare and correct animal husbandry.

My first visit to TOLFA came about after a local man saw me concerned for a stray that had been hit by a moped. (The dog was taken to the shelter, made a full recovery and was returned to his patch.) We got talking; he told me about TOLFA and offered to take me to have a look round. When we rode in and were greeted by a pack of about twenty dogs – the shelter's permanent residents – I knew that I was going to like the place. I spent a month there alongside other volunteers, including Clara and the wonderful Serena. Serena, who took the photographs in this section of the book, has returned over and over again to help at TOLFA, giving up a career as a producer to do so.

My main job at the shelter was to walk the dogs. For a stray, so used to freedom, being locked up in a kennel is especially bewildering. Half-an-hour outside – to feel the sand between their paws and put their noses to the breeze – would calm the dogs no end. It was something small I could offer them; after all, dogs have given me so much.

While volunteering, I witnessed an array of illnesses and afflictions, from skin diseases to injuries caused by other dogs, motor vehicles or humans. One such tragic, though unfortunately not isolated, case was of a stray that had had acid thrown over him. His burns were so bad that his tendons were exposed. With some TLC, aloe vera and time, however, this lovely natured dog made a full recovery.

There are those who would argue that spending time and money on animals is not right when there are so many humans in need of help. But, as Mohandas Gandhi, the 'Father of India', said, 'The greatness of a nation and its moral progress can be judged by the way its animals are treated.' My belief is that humans have a responsibility to other animals. As the most intelligent and powerful species on the planet, we have a duty to Earth and all its inhabitants. Animals

Rain, a Dutch volunteer, was passing through Pushkar and came to the shelter for a while to help with dog walking, feeding and general care of the resident animals.

give so much, from the donkey carrying rubble on the building site, the dutiful cow producing milk each day and the bullock ploughing the rice paddy to the playful puppy bringing simple pleasure to a child. We cannot take all this without giving something back.

As a dog lover, I found it a real joy to observe the strays behaving so naturally. The dynamics and politics of the pack are fascinating, the bonds between individuals so touching. This behaviour reminded me that dogs were dogs long before we brought them into our homes. The loyalty and affection that they show us stem from their instincts as pack animals to protect and care for their pack members.

Ramesh, with a temporary resident at the shelter, sits in the ABC (Animal Birth Control) kennels with a van full of sterilized and vaccinated dogs behind him, ready to go back to the street.

I learned so much spending time around these dogs, trying to capture them on film. Sometimes I ventured too close to unwilling participants and received some serious warnings to back off, which I had to do no matter how good the photo opportunity. So many times, however – in fact, on a daily basis – I would befriend an individual or a group, feed them a little, photograph them and share a satisfying moment of tenderness between human and canine.

I would spend several hours each day walking around, waiting and hoping for dogs to perform for my camera. I would look for dogs in interesting or unusual situations, leading me to some pretty awful locations. I got so many odd looks from the locals as I traipsed across a rubbish dump or down a seedy back alley in search of a shot. I'm sure most of them thought I was completely mad. But through my explorations of these unlikely and off-the-beaten-track sites, I truly discovered India. Through the dogs and my photography, my eyes were opened to a whole country and its people, to a different way of life – a wonderful way of life.

I spent a year in India. The country and its people enchanted me, and the dogs I came across did nothing but reinforce my devotion to these sensitive, beautiful and most charming of creatures.

The grounds of TOLFA's shelter near the start of the monsoon season: the land is transformed from barren dust to lush greenery in a matter of weeks.

Street Life

Rachel Wright

For me, the life of a street dog in India is one of freedom and the ability to live as nature intended: hanging around all day with your mates, scavenging for food, defending your territory and competing with other dogs to find a mate, thus ensuring the survival of the fittest. All this is natural behaviour for a dog, and when I have to return to the UK to work as a veterinary nurse, it's something that I feel we have taken away from our pets.

In our naive love for our special canines, we have frequently isolated them from the pack. We have created unnatural territories that cause anxiety for our dogs as they try to defend them. We give them commercial diets, synthesized beyond all recognition from the original produce, and the dogs are not required to use brain power to obtain food. Natural selection rarely exists, as two dogs are forced to mate in order to continue attributes that are so often cosmetic rather than geared to health or survival, simply because that is what the human 'owner' desires. In my mind, our actions have created so many confused and malformed dogs, and it breaks my heart to see them.

I am fortunate enough, however, to witness the lives of Indian street dogs on a daily basis and, for the most part, I think that they are contented. As morning breaks, each dog wakes up and greets his fellow pack members with face licks and tail wags. He plays a game of chase, lurching on his opponent until he rolls on his back in submission. He then finds a cool spot in which to sleep away the midday sun, ready for the night's activity, when he uses his ingenuity to catch his prey. He has the freedom to do what he as a dog wishes to do. So often, that freedom dictates that the street dog 'chooses' to live in symbiosis with his human cohabitants. He understands the benefits of close contact with humans.

The stray dogs can be divided into two very distinct groups: those that are fully feral and do not want to come into contact with humans, and those that are semi-feral or community dogs, thriving on the human contact and the food that they receive. Of course, life is not all good, and there are many problems associated with the freedom that a stray enjoys. If a street dog becomes sick or is injured, who provides him with the care that is necessary for his recovery? Bite wounds turn septic and become infested with maggots; fractures caused by road accidents heal in peculiar positions, leading to deformity; and without vaccination programmes, the diseases that we have eradicated in the West are commonplace and frequently fatal. Out of an average litter of six puppies, one or two are likely to survive, and a street dog is lucky to live to the age of five.

Two dogs keep lookout from a roof in Mandvi, in the state of Gujarat.

Street dogs are integral to the ecosystem of the Indian streets, and I would hate to see them disappear. Anyone who has visited India will know that rubbish is an ever-present sight. The dogs have a role in reducing the amount of that perishable rubbish, as well as keeping down the rat population. Research has shown that the rat population exploded, causing widespread disease among humans, in an area where the street dogs were

Local children and men mingle with dogs on the beach at Puri, Orissa.

exterminated over a short period of time. If the rubbish situation were to improve, I am sure that the dog population would slowly diminish of its own accord, owing to the removal of two of its available food sources. Perhaps then the continual human–animal conflict would not exist.

Not everyone can see the beauty or charm of the dogs. To some people, they are a pest, a source of rabies and a threat to their children. Every day our animal shelter receives calls from members of the public about 'nuisance' or 'danger' dogs, which, when we arrive on the scene, are simply dogs going about their daily business. Humans have claimed the territory as 'theirs' and, not understanding the important role that dogs play in the community, have decided that the street dog is an unwelcome visitor.

The ever-present threat of rabies has a very damaging effect on the reputation of street dogs, and I think that will always be the case until this horrific disease has been eradicated. The fear of being bitten by a street dog is passed from one generation to the next. Sometimes this fear shows itself as total avoidance of the dogs, but so often it takes the form of violence. People throw stones, wield sticks or aim a deft kick in order to keep the dogs away.

A dog rests under a sign outside a store in Rishikesh, Uttarakhand.

Of course, these actions usually result in making the dogs more aggressive and prone to bite. These nonsensical actions actually encourage the very behaviour from the dogs that engenders fear in the first place.

If anything were to change to improve the lives of these beautiful, intelligent creatures, I think it would be for this cycle of violence to be broken. We must teach younger generations to replace reactionary behaviour with understanding and compassion. Treat others – humans and non-humans alike – as you would wish to be treated yourself.

Rachel Wright is the founder of Tree of Life for Animals (TOLFA), an animal hospital and shelter in Rajasthan.

Man's Best Friend

Varanasi

Udaipur

Varanasi

Varanasi

Darjeeling

This homeless man was never far away from these three dogs; they shared the same patch on the Calcutta streets. Every time I walked past, the man was alone, clearly preferring the company of dogs to that of humans.

Calcutta

Calcutta

Pushkar

Calcutta

Calcutta

This little dog became a favourite of mine. Despite having a twisted front leg and a large tumour on her hindquarters, she had the sweetest nature. Every day I fed her scraps from the butcher's and – as I became accustomed to doing for many dogs – saved her bits of my dinner. She slept on this market stall at night and hung around her small patch during the day. Most dogs are pack animals, but she was a loner. She gave me the fondest farewell on my last day in Darjeeling. It's sad to think that the tumour has probably taken her life by now.

Darjeeling

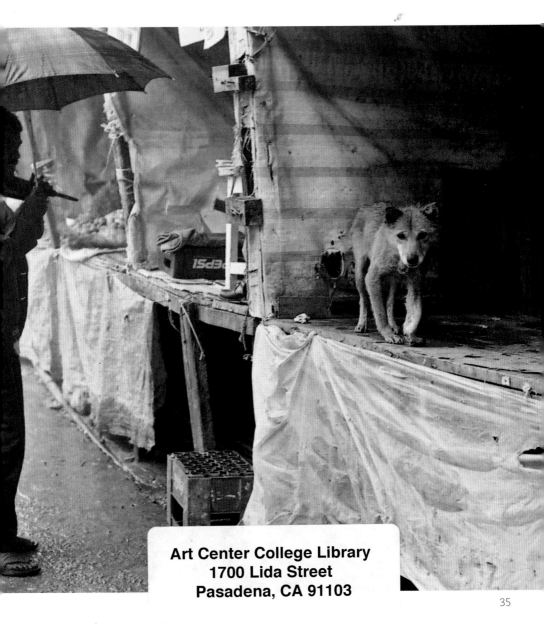

Darjeeling

Every chai stall – chai being the Indian cuppa – has its resident dog. The dogs hang around, waiting for scraps while making the most of the shelter and enjoying the company of regular visitors to the stalls.

Varanasi

Calcutta

Varanasi

Puri

Rishikesh

Specialist
Chamber:
Timing:
Except

Calcutta
47

Bodh Gaya

Varanasi

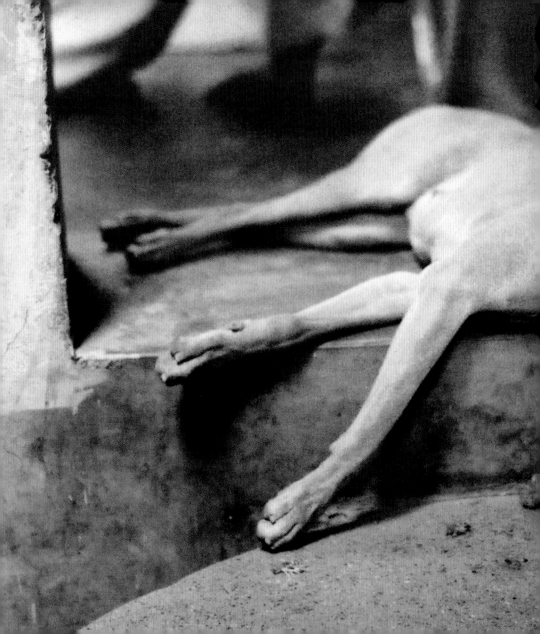

Let Sleeping Dogs Lie

Calcutta

Darjeeling

Darjeeling

In pre-monsoon India, temperatures regularly reach 45°C during the day. Dogs and humans alike keep cool any way they can. This pup dug a hole just big enough to wriggle into, covering his nearby mother in sand in the process. He was part of a large pack of dogs living on the banks of the River Ganges in Varanasi. At night an old man slept surrounded by the pack. Every day I came to feed the dogs and so we developed a friendship. The man spoke no English, but – as happened many times during my travels – our mutual compassion for dogs provided a common ground.

Varanasi

Varanasi

Hampi

Pushkar

माखू बीड़ी सिगरेट पीना मना है

भोजन करना मना है

Rishikesh

Darjeeling

Varanasi

Amritsar

The best patch imaginable for a street dog is one with a butcher's shop. This dog would sit faithfully outside this particular shop, patiently waiting for scraps. In this shot I think it looks like he is dreaming of ham and sausages!

Darjeeling

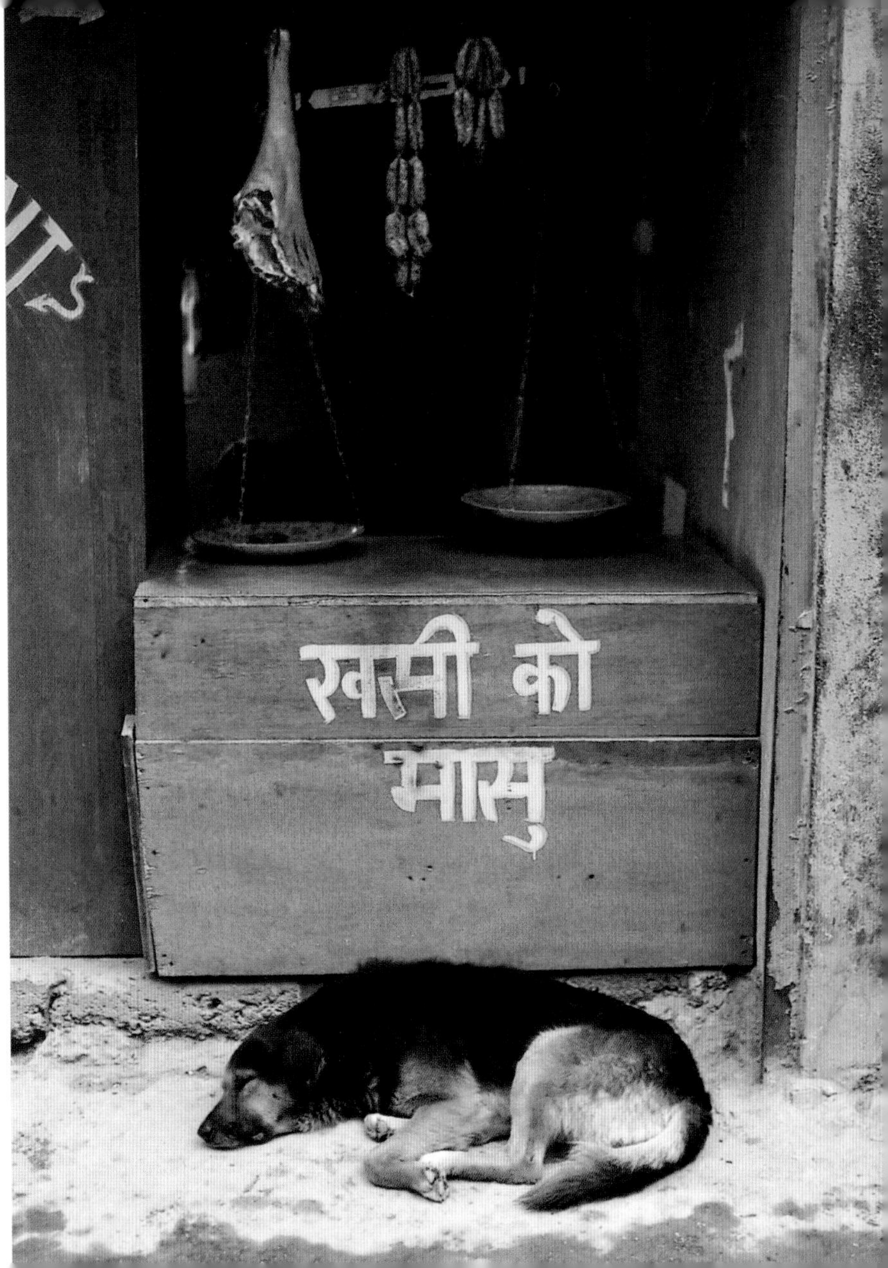
खसी को
मासु

Calcutta

Darjeeling

Varanasi

Udaipur

Jodhpur

Calcutta

Bhuj

Puri

Anything is a potential bed to a stray dog. Here, some tyre tracks provide a suitable place to rest a while.

Bodh Gaya

Pushkar

Diu

Puri

Calcutta

Calcutta

84

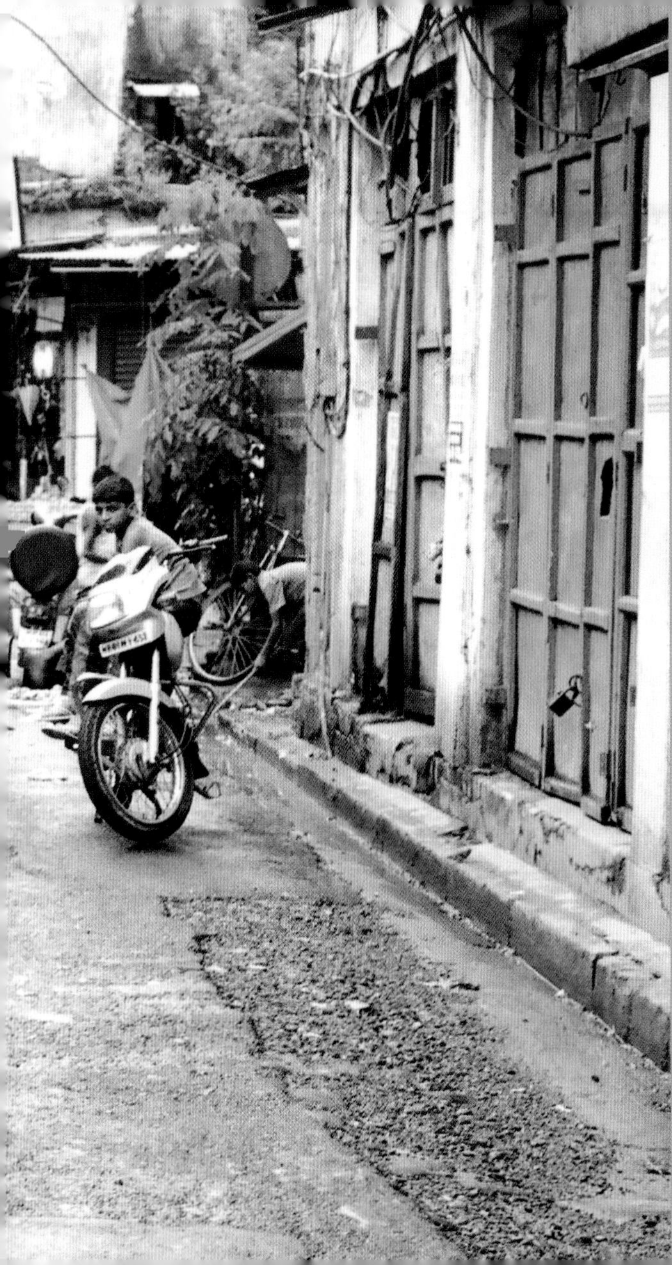

The Town Dog

This shot was taken on a busy street in Calcutta at my favourite time of day – first thing in the morning, just after the sun had risen. The real hustle and bustle of the day had not yet begun, and this dog could lie happily in the middle of the road (as dogs often do at night) and just let the world go by around him.

Calcutta

Varanasi

Calcutta

Calcutta

Rishikesh

Darjeeling

I was keen to experience all aspects of India, and I couldn't leave without witnessing the monsoon rains that arrive in June. The intensity of the rain is incredible, all the more so for the contrast it offers to the intense heat that envelops the country in the lead-up to the monsoon, when temperatures of 45°C are not uncommon. When the rain finally arrives, it brings huge relief: children frolic in the long-awaited water, while street-dwellers might take the opportunity for a good wash. In India, rain is seen as a gift from the gods, and it means the difference between life and death for the millions of inhabitants reliant on farming. It is something to be revered and celebrated. Drainage in most Indian towns and cities is rudimentary, and flooding often occurs. Everyone carries on with good humour, and as quickly as the floods appear, they are gone again.

Calcutta

Puri

Puri

Varanasi

Agra

Varanasi

Varanasi

Wherever there is a pile of sand or building material of any kind, you will usually find a dog on it. I think the dogs like being high up, and enjoy the softness the pile offers – a softness not easily found on the streets. They also use it as a kind of territorial marker: 'This is MY sand pile!'

Jalgaon

Delhi

Delhi

I used to refer to this street as 'Dog Alley', while a friend, Serena, called it 'Sweet Street'. Both names are wholly appropriate, as this place is home to a dozen or so stalls selling all manner of Indian sweets and to a pack of around fifteen dogs living off the scraps and leftovers. The stallholders are amazingly tolerant of these scavengers, possibly recognizing their benefit as ratters.

Udaipur

Pushkar

This rubbish dump in central Calcutta is a hive of activity for humans and animals alike. There is nothing that a stray relishes more than a large heap of rubbish. Dogs happily sit among the rag-pickers and rubbish, eating anything edible in sight.

Calcutta

Calcutta

Darjeeling

Darjeeling

One of the oldest Christian burial grounds in
the city, Park Street Cemetery is an oasis of
calm in frenetic Calcutta. The noise of the
traffic fades away and peace takes over the
place. This particular dog, one of a pack of
four (and a litter of tiny puppies), was the
self-appointed tour guide. He took us all
around the site, doing his rounds as he went.
The slightly eccentric workers at the cemetery
clearly loved and cared for these dogs.

Calcutta

Varanasi

Pushkar

Puri

Leh

The railway station is a focal point for every town in India, and the station in Darjeeling is especially important: it is the home of the world-famous Himalayan 'Toy Train', a narrow-gauge railway that is a relic of the British Raj. Steam trains first began making the journey from Siliguri to Darjeeling in the summer of 1881 and still run today. This majestic pair of dogs lived on and around the tracks of the historic station.

Darjeeling

The Country Dog

Munnar, in the southern state of Kerala, is in one of the principal tea-producing regions in India. The landscape is filled with woodland and tea fields shining green in the sun. The whole place exudes a sense of peace, which comes, I think, from being surrounded by so much vegetation. Whole communities have been established around the production of tea. The workers here (most of them come from Tamil Nadu) were some of the friendliest, most generous people I met.

Munnar

Darjeeling

Kodaikanal

134

Gokarna

Hampi, in Karnataka, is a UNESCO World Heritage site. The ancient town is littered with fourteenth-century ruins of beautifully intricate Hindu temples. This dog belonged to a pack comprising three adults and a litter of puppies; they lived in a remote group of ruined temples. I watched one day as the mother returned from a food-finding mission with a mouthful of tasty morsels. The welcome she received was emphatic, and the nervy pups forgot my presence on their mother's arrival.

Hampi

Hampi

Hampi

This shot was taken on a trip to neighbouring Sri Lanka. These women had come on to the rocks at sunset to sing and praise God, and the air reverberated with the sweet sound of their voices. The dog, in that way that dogs do, situated himself close enough to the action to enjoy the companionship of the women – but not too close.

Unawatuna, Sri Lanka

Munnar

Ghum

This motley crew captured my heart. Each dog looks so different from the others, I have no idea how they came to be a pack at all. I had seen the small black pup roaming alone, not too far away, a few days previously. He had obviously found himself among these other misfits and was accepted into the fold. A lovely teenage girl, who helped run the small shop just out of shot, cared for and fed the dogs. Her favourite was the shaggy beige one, whom she named 'Beeny'.

Darjeeling

Darjeeling

Alleppey

The Manali–Leh Highway, connecting the towns of Manali and Leh in northernmost India, is open only between June and mid-September, weather permitting. The route crosses breathtaking Himalayan scenery. This dog was at a stop we made at a dhaba (a roadside eatery) in a remote location. He was a shy fellow but didn't mind my presence as long as I kept my distance. He appears to be doing his best to look proud and commanding against such an imposing and majestic backdrop.

Manali–Leh Highway

Gokarna

Gokarna

Rishikesh

Varanasi

Varanasi

154

I followed this dog for some time as I waited for a train. He appeared to have a lust for life, and trotted alone up the platform, sniffing as he went. Every railway station in India has its dogs. The stations provide shelter and, with hordes of people passing through, there is usually food to be found.

Gokarna

Rishikesh

If I could have brought one dog home from India, it would have been Edge – so called for his slightly strange personality and edginess, which we soon discovered were due to the flea infestation in his lustrous fur. This shot was taken on one of our long walks together; Edge followed us wherever we went and slept outside our room. Using omelette as bait (one thing I discovered on my travels is that a dog will do almost anything for an egg), my long-suffering boyfriend and I washed and scrubbed him clean of his parasites – a process he did not enjoy one bit. Edge lost his edge after that and became a different dog, free from the irritation of fleas. I say that I would have brought him home with me, but what Edge loved most of all was the freedom to roam his patch, coaxing food and affection from tourists with his winning personality.

Rishikesh

Ghum

Diu

Diu

164

Mandvi

Puri

166

Mandvi

Puri

Mange – a parasitic skin disease that causes irritation, inflammation and loss of fur – is a common affliction among stray dogs. This little guy had the most beautiful eyes, shining out from his patchy, saggy skin. Unfortunately, because mange is highly contagious, many strays on this stretch of beach were affected.

Puri

Mandvi

Mandvi

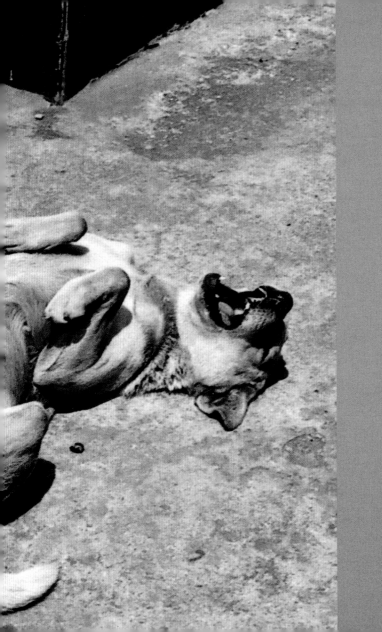

It's a Dog's Life

Rishikesh

We had just turned a corner on one of our daily walks in cold, misty Darjeeling when my boyfriend suddenly exclaimed, in hushed tones, 'Eloo, cat sitting on a dog!' And there they were, outside a house, keeping each other warm. I saw many cats and dogs sharing company in India, although the dogs greatly outnumber the cats.

Darjeeling

McLeodganj

Puri

Calcutta

184

Calcutta

186

Darjeeling

Pushkar

Pushkar

Varanasi

Rishikesh

In India, dogs share the streets with cows, sacred animals in Hinduism. The resulting relationship between the two species is largely one of indifference. But some dogs, seemingly in recognition that cows rule supreme in India, buddy up with their counterparts. I even witnessed a cow grooming a dog, licking him clean. Unfortunately, by the time I got my camera ready, the cow had stopped, almost – it seemed – out of embarrassment.

Puri

Puri

194

Mandvi

Varanasi

Bodh Gaya

Vashisht

Pushkar

Darjeeling

200

Darjeeling

This atmospheric image was taken just before a storm, when there was electricity in the air. These dogs had just been fighting with another pack (more snarling than actual fighting), and they had come to regroup here, on what was clearly their patch.

Puri

Varanasi

Mandvi

Puri

Raja was given his name by the group of men who worked on the beach in his patch. The men had taught him to give paw, which he did with unremitting enthusiasm. He was a lovely, very sweet-natured dog, who had clearly benefited from befriending the group. The scars on his face are a common sight among older male dogs; they are evidence of fighting over territory and the company of females.

Darjeeling

Darjeeling

Pushkar

Udaipur

214

Varanasi

Chandipur

One day on the beach at Puri, eastern India, I came across an unusually large number of howling dogs; the exact cause of their behaviour remains a mystery. These two dogs were sitting paw to paw, totally engrossed in their howling. They were virtually oblivious to me standing a couple of metres away, pointing my camera at them. I adore the sound of howling: it encapsulates 'dog-ness' so well. It takes dogs back to their primal selves, and evokes a similar feeling within me.

Puri

Charities and Other Organizations

World Society for the Protection of Animals (WSPA)
wspa-international.org
wspa.org.uk

The WSPA works internationally to improve the welfare of animals and to end cruelty towards them. It achieves positive results for wildlife and companion and farm animals through fieldwork, disaster relief, education and campaigns to improve legislation and build awareness. By bringing together the energies of more than nine hundred member organizations from around the world, WSPA is creating a powerful, unified animal welfare movement

People for the Ethical Treatment of Animals (PETA)
peta.org
peta.org.uk

With more than two million members and supporters, PETA is the largest animal rights organization in the world. PETA focuses its attention on the suffering of animals in factory farms, in laboratories, in the clothing trade and in the entertainment industry, but it also works on a variety of other issues, including campaigning to stop the barbaric mass destruction of street dogs in India. PETA works through public education, cruelty investigations, research, animal rescue, legislation, special events, celebrity involvement and protest campaigns.

International Animal Rescue (IAR)
internationalanimalrescue.org

IAR adopts a hands-on approach to the rescue and rehabilitation of suffering wild and domestic animals. Its main campaigns focus on freeing dancing bears, rescuing primates from animal smugglers, saving migratory birds from being shot, and providing veterinary care for stray dogs and cats in India. It has a rescue centre in Goa called Animal Tracks.

Four Paws UK
fourpaws.org.uk

With offices in nine European countries, Four Paws is an international charity that promotes rights for abused animals. It champions the notion that every animal has the right to be treated with consideration and to live a life with dignity that complies with its needs. Its campaigns are wide-ranging, and include the care of stray animals, particularly in Eastern Europe.

A portion of the proceeds will be donated to Tree of Life for Animals (TOLFA)

Tree of Life for Animals (TOLFA)
tolfa.org.uk

TOLFA runs an animal hospital and shelter based between Ajmer and Pushkar in the state of Rajasthan. It aims to rescue, treat, care and rehabilitate animals, especially strays, suffering from injury, disease, maltreatment or ill-use, and to help eradicate those diseases such as rabies that can be transmitted between animals and humans. By educating people on all aspects of animal welfare, TOLFA works to foster compassion towards our fellow sentient beings. TOLFA also runs an effective sterilization and vaccination programme, which has treated some 10,000 dogs since its inception in 2005.

Anand Chhaaya (Shelter of Happiness)
anandchhaaya.org

Established in 1997, Anand Chhaaya is an animal welfare organization set up with the primary aim of humanely controlling the stray-dog population in Bangalore, Karnataka, through the Animal Birth Control (ABC) programme. It also runs an animal shelter that accommodates abandoned or injured dogs.

Animal Aid Unlimited
animalaidunlimited.com

Animal Aid runs an animal hospital and shelter in Udaipur, Rajasthan, where sick and injured street animals are treated before being returned to the community. Animal Aid sterilizes several thousand dogs a year and vaccinates them against rabies. It also runs an educational programme for local people, encouraging responsible animal husbandry and concern for animal welfare.

Animal Welfare Board of India
awbi.org

The Animal Welfare Board was set up in 1962 in accordance with the Prevention of Cruelty to Animals Act of 1960, with the object of advising the government of India on all matters associated with animal welfare. The board supports the ABC system of controlling dog populations.

Help in Suffering (HIS-India)
his-india.org.au

HIS runs three animal shelters in India: two in Jaipur, in the state of Rajasthan; the other in Kalimpong, West Bengal. Initially established with funding from the WSPA, the HIS ABC programme has been running since 1994 and is proof that street-dog populations do stabilize. The programme has helped create a friendly, rabies-free street-dog population in Jaipur, providing a template for other municipalities to follow.

India Project for Animals and Nature (IPAN)
indiapan.org

Established in 1997 in Nilgiris, Tamil Nadu, IPAN is dedicated to preventing animal cruelty, improving the health and welfare of domestic and wild animals, protecting the environment and, by so doing, enhancing the livelihood of people depending on the animals' well-being. It runs an animal hospital and shelter, a sterilization programme, an education programme and street clinics for working horses, donkeys and ponies.

The Welfare of Stray Dogs (WSD)
wsdindia.org

WSD is a Mumbai-based organization that works to eradicate rabies and to control the street-dog population through humane, effective methods. It also aims to educate the public about rabies prevention and other stray-dog issues. WSD promotes the adoption of stray dogs as pets within the city of Mumbai, Maharashtra.

To all the people and dogs who enriched my life every day in India. And for Jamie, whose patience and understanding know no bounds – thank you

Eloise Leyden grew up in Bournemouth, on the south coast of England, and graduated with a degree in photography from the University of Plymouth in 2006. *Slum Dogs of India*, her first book, resulted from a year-long trip to the subcontinent. Since returning to England, she has adopted a rescue dog.

For more information and for enquiries about print sales and pet portraiture, visit **eloiseleyden.co.uk**

First published 2009 by

Merrell Publishers Limited
81 Southwark Street
London SE1 0HX

merrellpublishers.com

British Library Cataloguing-in-Publication Data:
Leyden, Eloise.
Slum dogs of India.
1. Feral dogs – India – Pictorial works.
2. India – Social conditions – Pictorial works.
I. Title
636.7'00954'0222-dc22

ISBN 978-1-8589-4504-0

Produced by Merrell Publishers Limited
Designed by Nicola Bailey
Project-managed by Claire Chandler
Printed and bound in China

Back cover: Rishikesh (top and centre);
  Calcutta (bottom)
Page 2: Varanasi; page 4: Varanasi;
pages 18–19: Rishikesh; pages 50–51: Varanasi;
pages 86–87: Calcutta; pages 128–29: Puri;
pages 176–77: Darjeeling